POO AT THE ZOO

SARAH EASON

Published in 2011 by
Bloomsbury Publishing PLC
50 Bedford Square, London, WC1B 3DP

www.bloomsbury.com

ISBN HB 978-1-4081-6050-3
PB 978-1-4081-7189-9

Manufactured and supplied under licence from the Zoological Society of London.

A CIP catalogue for this book is available from the British Library.

Produced for Bloomsbury Publishing by Calcium. www.calciumcreative.co.uk

Illustrated by Kirsten Collier

Printed in China by C&C Offset Printing Co.

CONTENTS

A zoo full of poo 4
Dragon poo 6
Doo-doo domain 8
Stink bomb 10
Anyone for poo? 12
Splats in space 14
A poo to be proud of 16
Call the cleaners 18
Creepy poos 20
Cat splats 22
Dainty doo-doo 24
Feeling peckish? 26
Splat facts 28
Glossary 30
ZSL London Zoo 31
Index 32

A ZOO FULL OF POO

From safari parks to city zoos, keepers everywhere are kept busy feeding their furry, scaly, big, tiny, cute and terrifying animals. As everyone knows, what goes in must come out, and that means doo-doo – lots of it. Shovels at the ready!

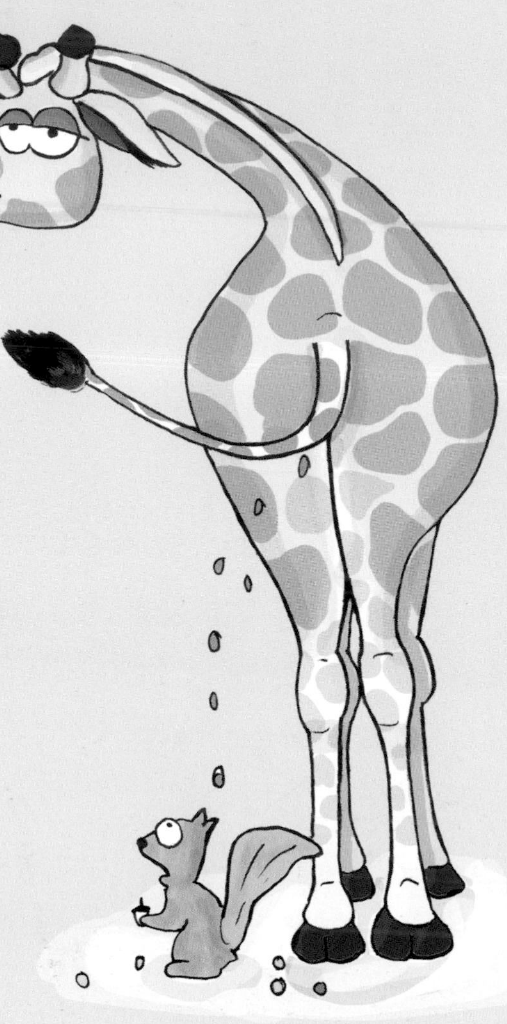

Power to the poop

So what happens to all the poo after it's been pooped? Some zoos sell it as manure – poo is packed with minerals and vitamins that help plants to grow. Others use splats to generate energy – poopy power! To get the full scoop on poop, let's take a look at the wildest doo-doo producers on Earth. Welcome to the zoo...

Did you know?

Some zoos have to shovel their way through half a million kilograms of poo every year – phoo-ey!

DRAGON POO

Komodo dragons do pretty smelly poos, but they have even stinkier breath. The mouth of a Komodo dragon is full of deadly, poisonous saliva – just one bite can kill its prey.

Did you know?

Komodo dragons trail their prey after they have bitten it – and wait for the animal to slowly die.

Poo protection

Komodo dragons will make a meal of almost anything – including their own babies! To keep safe, baby dragons cover themselves in poo – pretty much the only thing an adult Komodo won't eat!

Poo? I'll pass...

If a Komodo dragon is really hungry, it will eat almost all of its prey – leaving just 10 per cent untouched! It will happily chew up hooves and bones, and even eat the intestines – once it's shaken them free of any poo inside, of course...

WHOPPER MEAL

The Komodo dragon is the only lizard that can kill prey bigger than itself, and bigger than it can swallow whole.

DOO-DOO DOMAIN

Want to walk on the wild side? Make sure it's not on a painted dog's patch – it's covered in doggy doo-doos.

Poopy patches

In the wild, painted dogs live in Africa. They mark out their territory with plops that warn other animals to stay away. Their smelly markers are packed with animal remains – these wild dogs eat just about anything they find. Gazelle, warthog, zebra, wildebeest, impala, springbok and young antelopes are all on the menu.

FAST FOOD

African hunting dogs can run at speeds of 66 kph (that's as fast as a car) to catch their prey. They tear flesh off their kill – then eat it while the animal is still alive...

Lovin' leftovers

A painted dog can't resist leftovers and will happily polish off the remains of their prey (bones and all). And zoo dogs love it when their keepers throw them a carcass. Tasty!

Did you know?

Only the pack leader is allowed to cock its leg to wee. Other dogs must wee with all four legs on the ground.

STINK BOMB

Note - never make a spider monkey mad. It might look cute, but if this furball of fun gets angry, it will splatter you with poo!

Take that!

Spider monkeys use their poo as missiles if they are cross – and because they spend most of their time up high in the trees, you're an easy target. If you're lucky, you might get a warning first – spider monkeys bark and scream when they are excited and the sound can be heard 1,000 metres away.

SNACK ATTACK

If monkeys get really hungry, they sometimes eat eggs they find in treetop nests and even spiders.

Pooing for the planet

Spider monkeys love eating fruit – in fact, 90 per cent of their diet is made up of it. They might not know it, but when they poo, spider monkeys are doing their bit for Planet Earth. Hundreds of fruit seeds in the poo are dropped onto the ground – and then spring up into new trees. High five for monkey poo!

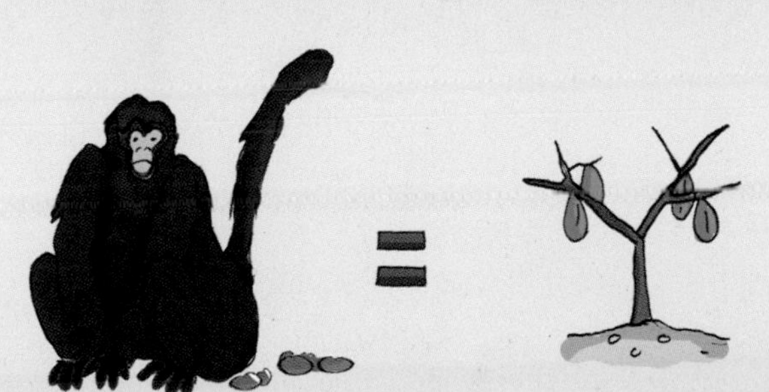

ANYONE FOR POO?

Camel poo is super-handy. It can be burned for fire, eaten for lunch and even swallowed to cure a stomach ache. Pass the poo, please...

Pop a poo pill

Think you've tasted the worst medicine on Earth? Think again! Nomadic Arabs used to pop a freshly-pooped pellet every time they had a tummy ache – and it worked! A chemical in the poo kills infection in the gut, stopping sickness in its tracks.

Strictly veggie?

Plant-loving camels are veggies by nature – they love their greens and will chomp on grass, leaves, bark and shoots. Sometimes, hungry camels snack on meat and fish. And really peckish camels will even eat tents, clothes and shoes. Luckily, what goes in always comes out…

Did you know?

Nomads have burned camel poo for fuel on fires for centuries.

MEAL DEAL

The dung beetle owes everything to camel poo. It eats only poo and without the camel's poopy food parcels, it could not survive in the desert.

SPLATS IN SPACE

Penguin poo has really made its mark on the planet – you can even see it from space. Respect!

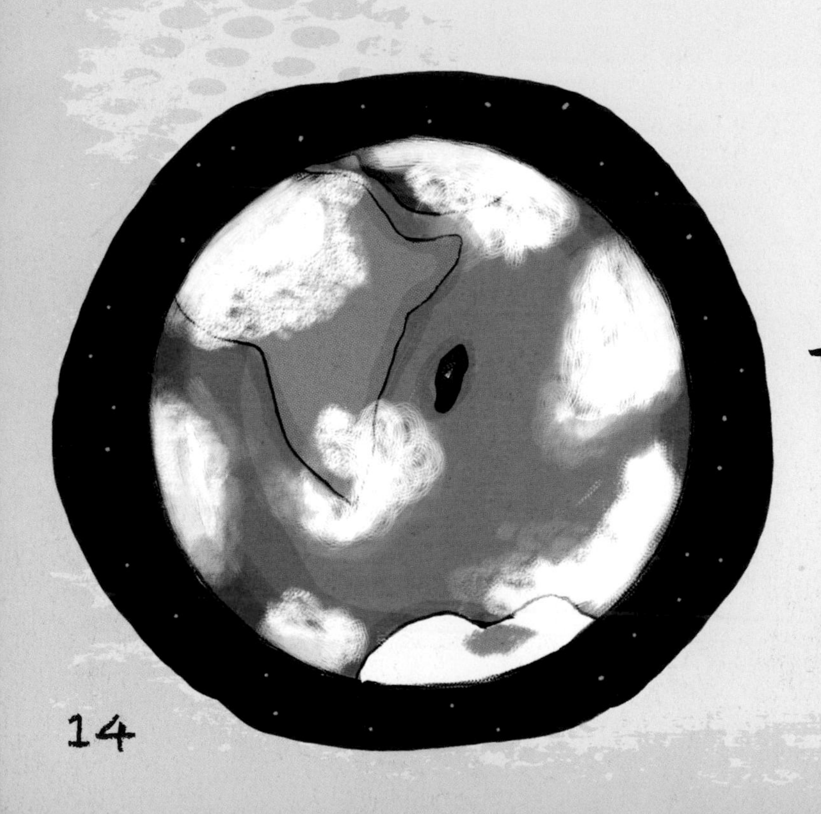

Planet Poop

Okay, so one penguin poo might not make much of a difference. But penguins live in colonies of thousands – and what do thousands of birds make? That's right – zillions of poos. The birdy plops turn huge areas of sea-ice brown, so scientists looking at the Earth from space can tell where the penguin colonies are.

Get a grip

Keeping your lunch down can be tricky for a penguin – their seafood diet is slippery stuff. Luckily, penguins have a hook at the end of their bills for grabbing food. They also have backward-facing bristles on their tongues that help them to grip food in their mouths.

SALTWATER COCKTAIL

Penguins are one of the few animals that can drink saltwater. A special gland in their body removes any salt in the water.

Did you know?

Penguin poo is called 'guano'.

A POO TO BE PROUD OF

You may have heard that lions are proud beasts – and so they should be. The big cat produces the stinkiest, smelliest poo of all the creatures at the zoo.

Did you know?

Not only are lions scary, so is their poo! Some people put it in their garden to frighten off domestic cats and foxes.

Talking poo

A lion's whiffy whoppers come in handy too – lions use them to mark out their territory. They smear the black, sticky stuff onto trees, bushes and rocks to tell other lions 'Back off, this is my stinky pad!'

The lion king (of poo)

So, how do lions make such super-stinky poo? It's all down to the amount of meat they eat. A male lion eats about seven kilograms of meat (about 27 burgers) each day. That's a lot of meat! Poo from meat-eating animals is always much stinkier than poo from plant-eating animals, so when you think about the amount of meat that goes into a lion's tummy, it's no surprise that their poopy piles are Top of the Plops!

ON A LION DIET

African lions can go without food for more than a week, and usually eat only every three or four days.

CALL THE CLEANERS

Pygmy hippos are not house-proud. These pint-sized poopers have an especially dirty habit – they twirl their tail when they poo to flick it everywhere!

Did you know?

When hippos flick their poo it is called a 'poop shower'.

Check out my poop pad

Pygmy hippos spread their muck when they poo to mark their territory. The splattered poo tells other pygmy hippos 'You're in *my* pygmy pad – so go away!'

Midnight feast

Pygmy hippos love a lie-in – they spend a lot of the day sleeping. They get up in the late afternoon to start looking for food and chomp away on leaves, plants and fruit until midnight.

DO NOT DISTURB!

Hippos spend a lot of time on the toilet – they poo twice as much as an elephant every day.

CREEPY POOS

Guess how smelly an anteater's poo is? It is so stinky that even the anteater can't stand the smell – they do it straight into water to try to cover it up. Phoo-ey!

Did you know?

A giant anteater can flick its tongue 150 times a minute. Impressive!

The termitator

Anteaters just love munching on termites – in fact, they can chomp their way through 166,000 of these minibeasts every single day. And if any of the little critters make a run for it, the anteater just stretches out its super-long tongue and terminates the termite.

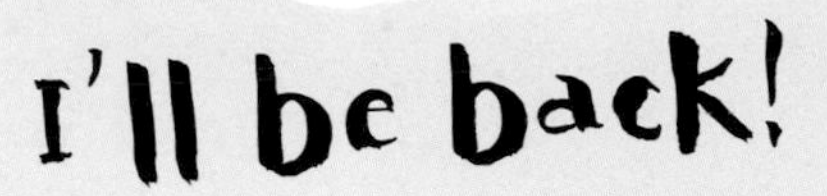

Anteaters don't completely destroy a termite mound in just one go. They leave some of the termites to rebuild their colony – so the anteater can go back later for seconds.

SNOOZE NEWS

Anteaters sleep for about 18 hours a day. Munching minibeasts is so exhausting!

The Sumatran tiger is the last tiger in Indonesia – and scientists are on a poop hunt to find out just how many are left in the wild.

Follow that poo!

Scientists record tiger poo to try to work out how many tigers may still be alive in the wild. Luckily for them, tiger poos are easy to spot – they are the size of a beetroot and have a strong, musky smell. Tigers also leave behind another handy calling card – their wee smells of freshly-cooked rice!

Eating out, eating in

Wild Sumatran tigers can eat about three deer in just one day. They hunt deer, wild boar and tapir. When they make a kill, they gorge themselves on the flesh and then don't eat again for days. Deer is not on the menu for zoo tigers – they are mainly fed rabbits by their keepers.

Did you know?

Tiger poo is called 'scat'.

DAINTY DOO-DOO

Despite being the tallest animal on Earth (the average male giraffe is three times taller than a man), giraffes are pretty dainty when it comes to poo.

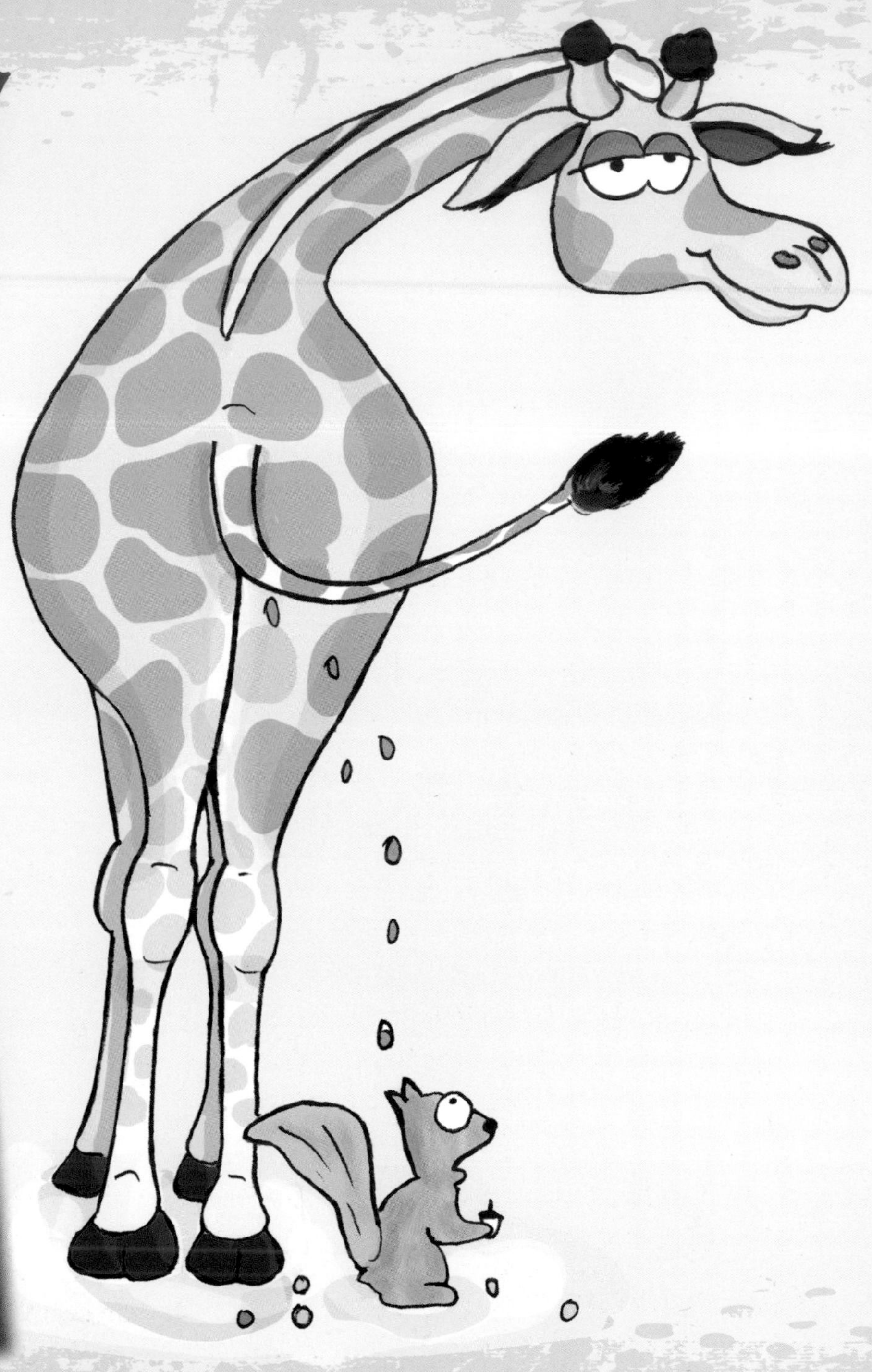

Did you know?

Food has to travel a *really* long way before it gets anywhere near a giraffe's stomach – its neck alone is as long as a human adult.

Pint-sized poop

Giraffes can eat huge amounts of leaves and twigs every day. You might think that would mean huge dollops of poo, but giraffe poo is actually quite small – each poo is only about the size of an olive. Tidy!

SPIT IT OUT!

The Kung people from the Kalahari desert in Africa play a giraffe dung-spitting game. Fun, huh?!

Amazing Acacia

A giraffe pulls leaves and twigs off its favourite tree, the Acacia tree, with its 18-cm-long tongue. Amazingly, giraffes take in so much water from the leaves that they can go for weeks without drinking.

It's best not to get up close and personal with a gorilla – they have a habit of eating their own poo!

Did you know?

An average gorilla poo is the size of a cola can.

vitasplats!

Gorillas love fruits, leaves, stems, seeds and even flowers. But if they are feeling under the weather, they eat their own poo. Gorilla poo is full of vitamins and minerals that gorillas need to stay healthy – and sometimes they even eat the poo of other animals for an extra protein punch.

EAT UP!

Gorillas chomp through at least five kilograms a day. Of plants, not poo - phew!

Poo in the bed

Gorillas make a new nest every night. That's because they do a poo in it every morning. Time for some toilet training…

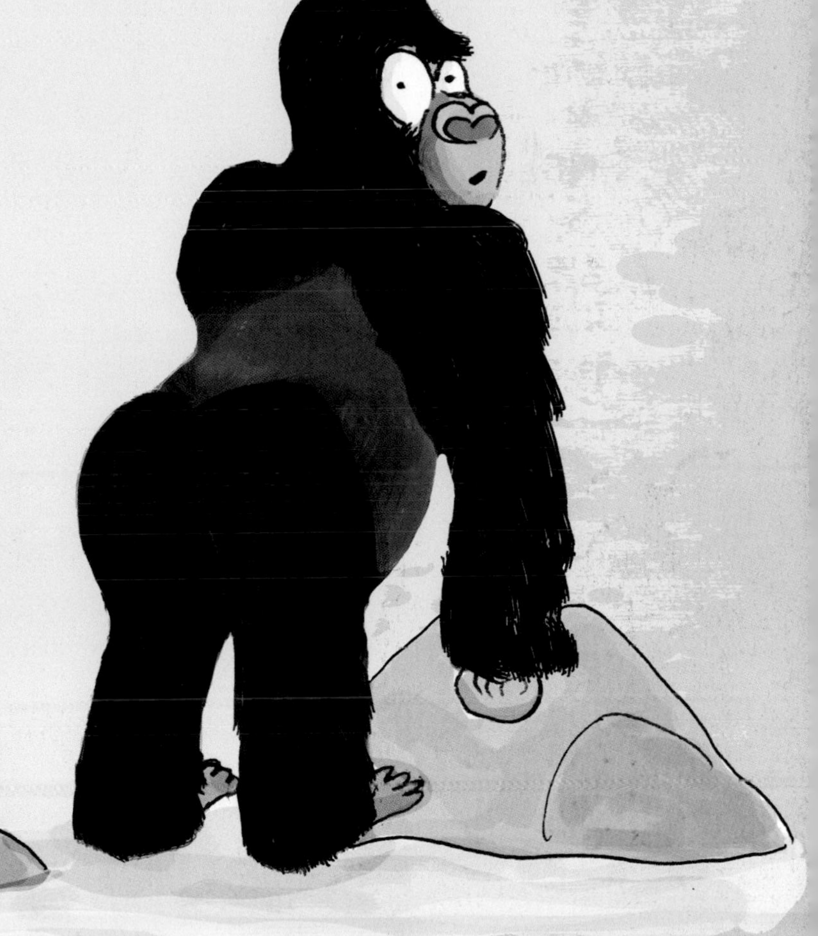

SPLAT FACTS

In some parts of Asia, coffee is made from beans swallowed by lemurs, then taken from their poo! It's expensive, too – just one cup costs £50.

Some animals eat their own poo! The poo contains minerals and vitamins that their bodies need.

Rabbits can do up to 500 poos a day.

The bacteria in poo makes it smell.

Blue whales do the biggest poos on the planet. An average poo can be 25 cm wide and several metres long. If the whales have been feeding on shrimp, their poos turn pink!

Lions only poo every three days.

Hippos follow their trail of dung poo at night to help them find their way around in the dark.

Bird poo is white because birds don't wee. Their uric acid is passed out with their poo, instead of their wee. The acid makes the poo white.

Mayflies are the only creature to never, ever poo. They live for just one day so must mate quickly – that means they don't have time to eat or poo.

Every couple of weeks, sloths climb down from the trees to poo on the ground. This is to stop the noise of a poopy splat landing from high above, which might attract the attention of a predator.

In Australia, people use tiger poo to scare roaming deer away from gardens.

You can buy paper that has been made of animal poo!

GLOSSARY

bacteria tiny organisms that can only be seen under a microscope

carcass the body of a dead animal

colonies groups of animals or insects

dung animal poo

gorge to eat until the stomach is completely full

impala a deer-like animal

Indonesia a country in Asia

minerals nutrients in food that the body needs for good health

nomadic always moving, never staying in one place

predator an animal that hunts other animals for food

prey an animal that is hunted and eaten by other animals

protein a substance found in food that provides energy and helps to build muscle

saltwater water that contains salt. Saltwater is found in the sea, freshwater is found in rivers and lakes

seafood fish and animals that live in the sea and that are eaten by other animals

springbok a deer-like animal

tapir a pig-like animal with a short snout

termites small, ant-like insects

territory an area marked out by an animal as its home

uric acid a strong substance found in bird poo and human wee

veggie short for vegetarian. An animal that does not eat meat

vitamins nutrients in food that the body needs for good health

warthog a pig-like animal with sharp, curved tusks. Warthogs live only in Africa

wild boar a pig-like animal with sharp, curved tusks. Wild boars are found worldwide

wildebeest large, plant-eating animals that live in herds in Africa

ZSL LONDON ZOO

The Zoological Society of London (ZSL) is a charity that provides help for animals at home and worldwide. We also run ZSL London Zoo and ZSL Whipsnade Zoo.

By buying this book, you have helped us raise money to continue our work with animals around the world.

Find out more at zsl.org

ZSL
LONDON
ZOO

ZSL
WHIPSNADE
ZOO

INDEX

animal remains 7, 8, 9, 23

bird poo 14, 15, 29

city zoos 4
cleaning up poo 4, 5
colour of poo 14, 17, 29

dung 13, 25, 29

eating poo 12, 13, 26, 27, 28

food and feeding 4, 6, 7, 8, 9, 11, 12, 13, 15, 17, 19, 21, 23, 24, 25, 26, 27, 28, 29

manure 5
marking territory with poo 8, 17, 19
minerals in poo 5, 27, 28

poo for fuel 5, 13
poo for medicine 12
poo names 15, 23
poo sizes 14, 23, 25, 26, 28
protein in poo 27

rolling in poo 7

safari parks 4
scientists and poo 14, 22, 23
seeds in poo 11
sickness 12
smells 5, 6, 8, 16, 17, 20, 23, 28

throwing poo 10, 11

using poo 5, 7, 10, 11, 12, 13, 16, 17, 19, 25, 27, 28, 29

vitamins in poo 5, 27, 28

wee 9, 23, 29